# PORTUGAL

An Imprint of Scholastic Library Publishing
Danbury, Connecticut

Published for Grolier
an imprint of Scholastic Library Publishing
Old Sherman Turnpike, Danbury, Connecticut 06816
by Marshall Cavendish Editions
an imprint of Marshall Cavendish International
1 New Industrial Road, Singapore 536196

Copyright © 2004 Times Media Pte Ltd, Singapore
Second Grolier Printing 2006

Set ISBN: 0-7172-5788-6
Volume ISBN: 0-7172-5799-1

**Library of Congress Cataloging-in-Publication Data**
Portugal.
p. cm.—(Fiesta!)
Summary: Discusses the festivals and holidays of Portugal and how the songs, food,
and traditions associated with these celebrations reflect the culture of the people.
1. Festivals—Portugal—Juvenile literature. 2. Portugal—Social life and customs—Juvenile literature.
[1. Festivals—Portugal. 2. Holidays—Portugal. 3. Portugal—Social life and customs.]
I. Grolier (Firm). II. Fiesta! (Danbury, Conn.)
GT4863.A2P67 2004
394.26469—dc21      2003044845

*For this volume*
Author: Leena Ng
Editor: Nafisah Ismail
Designer: Jailani Basari
Production: Nor Sidah Haron
Crafts and Recipes produced by Stephen Russell

Printed by Everbest Printing Co. Ltd

Adult supervision advised for all crafts and recipes,
particularly those involving sharp instruments and heat.

# CONTENTS

# PORTUGAL

*Portugal is a country with a rich seafaring past. Its amazing beauty and diversity, as well as its friendly people, are a source of inspiration for many.*

**ATLANT OCEAN**

▼ **Port wine** is part of Portugal's history. The famed sweetish red brandy is a signature of the country and is loved by lords and farmers alike, who drink it before meals. The best ports are produced around Porto (also known as Oporto to the Portuguese people). Porto is Portugal's second largest city and is situated at the mouth of the Duoro River.

▲ **The architecture** of Portugal is best described as Moorish with surrealist influence. The unique style and design of its buildings and monuments were developed all the way back in the 16th century. Portuguese architecture uses a lot of twists, turns, spirals, and nautical themes as decoration.

Minho

Moure/Braga/Barcelos

voa de Varzim

Guimarães

Porto

Duoro River

Ovar

Tagus

Coimbra

Fatima

Nazaré

Loulé

LISBON

Évora

**SPAIN**

Faro

Madeira

▲ **The melancholic fado** is a gentle, lyrical song believed to have originated from sailors in the 16th century. Fados are played at many religious festivals celebrated around the country, especially at *romarias*, which are pilgrimages held in honor of saints. They are often accompanied by traditional folk dancing and are popular in rural towns.

▲ **Bullfighting** in Portugal is neither as common nor as violent as in Spain. In a Portuguese *tourada* ("bullfight") the horseman (as a matador is known in Portugal) tries to make several stabs into the bull with his darts, but he pulls them out again. The bull is not killed during a Portuguese bullfight.

# RELIGIONS

***Most Portuguese are Roman Catholics. Various traditional Catholic festivals are celebrated throughout the year, a sign that the people are very religious.***

*Catholics believe that the infant Jesus, a child from God, was born to Mary and Joseph.*

Portugal has a lot of *romarias* (religious pilgrimages), *festas* (festivals), and *feiras* (fairs), which bring whole towns to a stop. There is at least one celebration almost every month.

Portugal is a very religious country, with more than 95 percent of the population being Roman Catholic. Traditional Catholic celebrations, processions, and pilgrimages are an important part of the lives of Portuguese.

It is believed that Catholicism first reached Portugal's southern coast around A.D. 1, when the Romans colonized the Mediterranean coast, which included Portugal and Spain. By the third century parishes were already set up in Braga (Portugal's religious capital), Évora, Faro, and Lisbon. Despite the arrival of new settlers from other parts of Europe, the Catholic faith remained strong in Portugal, since these foreigners were often quickly converted to become Catholics.

However, at the end of the 7th century the ruling kingdom

of Portugal became torn between two groups. One group asked for help from the Muslims in North Africa. In 711 the first Moors entered Spain and within 10 years controlled most of it. With the arrival of the Muslims, Islam and its practices were introduced to Portugal.

*Moorish reign in Portugal ended in the 12th century, but its influence remains, as seen in this Portuguese tile with a Moorish design.*

# GREETINGS FROM **PORTUGAL!**

Portuguese is the official language in the country. If you understand a little Spanish or French, you will not have much problem reading Portuguese. But the pronunciations of many Portuguese words are entirely different from the way they are read in English. Thankfully most people understand Spanish. French and English are widely spoken in major cities and tourist areas. The national costume of Portugal is the traditional dress worn by the women living in the Minho region of northwestern Portugal.

## How do you say...

Hello
**Olá**

Good morning
**Bom dia**

Good afternoon/goodnight
**Boa tarde**

Goodbye/see you later
**Adeus, até logo**

Thank you
**Obrigado**

Please
**Por favor**

# CARNAVAL

*Carnaval is celebrated all over Portugal in great spirits.*
*Streets are filled with streamers, firecrackers,*
*water pistols, and people dressed in fancy costumes.*

The month of February, which is the month before Lent, is known as *entrudo*. Elaborate celebrations for Carnaval ("goodbye to meat" in Spanish) are held to observe abstinence from meat for Roman Catholics during this time.

Carnaval festivities take place in many of the country's major towns and cities, notably in Nazaré,

*Dancers in street processions wear colourful costumes and fancy masks like these.*

*Partygoers enjoy food and wine during Carnaval and hold open-air sardine roasts.*

Ovar, Loulé, and Funchal (Madeira). Each town has its own way of celebrating the occasion, but all towns have colorful processions, dances, and street parties known as *arraiais*. The towns are seldom quiet because firecrackers are set off throughout the day.

The street processions are held at squares or in open spaces decorated with lights and are open to everyone. The programs

are lined up for the three days, and the celebrations at Loulé are particularly lively. There are about 100 dancers marching through the streets each evening. Beside them are colorful floats decorated with flowers. The high point is the choosing of the Carnaval Queen. The contestants wear very elaborate costumes with headdresses. The winner of the contest has the honor of opening the festivities the next year.

# MAKE A CARNAVAL MASK

### YOU WILL NEED
*Colored card*
*Glittery pipe cleaners*
*Crépe paper*
*Adhesive stars*
*Wooden skewer or garden stake*
*PVA glue & brush*
*Glue stick*
*A pair of glasses, preferably oval-shaped ones*
*Paper doily*

**1** Place the glasses onto the card, and draw around them with a pencil. Add to your outline fancy curves on both sides of the mask. Cut out the final shape with scissors.

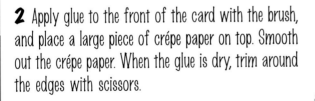

**2** Apply glue to the front of the card with the brush, and place a large piece of crépe paper on top. Smooth out the crépe paper. When the glue is dry, trim around the edges with scissors.

**3** Fold the paper doily in half, and cut in half following the fold line. Glue one half of the doily to the back of the mask with paper glue. The cut-out semicircle should be positioned  in the center of the mask with its arch sticking out. Draw eyeholes on the front of the mask, then cut them out.

**4** Stick colored paper or foil stars around the upper and outer edge of the masks.

**5** Ask an adult to trim any sharp ends from the wooden skewer or garden stake. Tightly wind pipe cleaners around the skewer to cover it completely. Stick the skewer to the back of the mask with PVA glue, and let dry thoroughly.

**6** Cut a rectangle piece of crépe paper, and wind a pipe cleaner around the middle to make a bow. Glue the bow onto the mask just above the eyeholes. Allow to dry. You can add sequins and glitter or even paint the doily.

# EASTER

*Processions and religious ceremonies take place all over Portugal during the Holy Week leading up to Easter. The event celebrates the death and resurrection of Jesus Christ and is observed by all Roman Catholics and Christians.*

All through Holy Week, which is in April, the people of Portugal hold festivities to mark one of the most respected occasions of the Roman Catholic and Christian faith.

These celebrations become greater as Good Friday draws near. On this day the entire nation breaks out in Easter cheer. Some of the most striking festivities take place in Póvoa de Varzim, Ovar, and especially Braga, which has processions featuring masked marchers and highly decorated floats along with fireworks, folk dancing, and torch parades. Hundreds of colorfully dressed believers march in these parades. On Good Friday crowds also gather in the town, wearing white hoods as a sign that they

*Altars in churches around the country usually have scenes of Christ from the Bible and are decorated with flowers and candles. Masses are held daily to offer prayers of thanks and worship.*

are sorry for their sins. They offer prayers to God and march through the streets carrying torches.

At some of the street processions in Braga and other towns children carry floats that they have made. Each float tells a story from the Bible.

In the evening Easter fireworks are set off to show that light comes out of darkness, and that new hope and life are born. The celebrations continue right to Easter Sunday, when big feasts are held after Mass.

*During the street processions boys carry a statue of Mary dressed in a black mourning dress. They are followed by girls wearing black dresses to reflect the death of Christ.*

## SACRED SUPPER

Sac-red sup-per means to die to who you are

and to leave be-hind the life that you've de-signed

to drink His blood, to taste His flesh, to

walk with Him in death, then to live the life that

on-ly He can give.

# FATIMA

***Portugal's most famous pilgrimage recalls
the appearance of Virgin Mary to three shepherd
children at Fatima. There are six annual pilgrimages
to this sacred site in remembrance of each of the
occasions Mary was seen.***

*In her appearances at Fatima to the
three shepherd children the Virgin
Mary repeatedly pointed out the
need to pray using the Rosary
daily, to wear the Brown Scapular
of Mount Carmel, and to perform
acts of reparation and sacrifice.*

Tens of thousands of pilgrims gather at the shrine of Our Lady of Fatima on the 13th of four months every year to mark the anniversary of the Virgin Mary's final appearance to three shepherd children in 1917. The first pilgrimage every year takes place in May, followed by others in August and September. The last pilgrimage falls in October.

Although the sighting was last believed to take place in 1917, it was only in 1930 that Fatima was authorized as a sacred pilgrimage site by the bishop of Leiria. Today, people from all over the world visit the shrine, which is situated 80 miles north of Lisbon. Many miracles of spiritual and physical healing have been attributed to Our Lady of Fatima. To show that they are thankful for all their answered prayers, pilgrims complete the final mile of

*In a religious procession worshippers
may hold lighted candles and follow a
statue of Mary that is decked in
flowers and carried around the church.*

their pilgrimage on their knees along a special walkway up to the shrine.

According to local legend, the Virgin Mary appeared six times to three shepherd children ("The Three Seers") near the town of Fatima between May 13 and October 13 in 1917. She told them that she had been sent by God with a message. At that time the world was torn by wars and violence. Mary promised that Heaven would grant peace to all the world if the believers prayed and obeyed her requests for reparation and also consecration.

The heart of Mary's message to the world is contained in what has come to be called the "Secret," which she told to the three seers during one of her appearances. The secret actually consists of three parts and is said to predict major events happening in the world.

*Pilgrims bring home Holy Water from Fatima in special bottles.*

# THE LEGEND OF THE ROOSTER

The people in Barcelos were disturbed by a crime and did not know who was responsible. When a stranger from Galica in northern Spain passed through their area, they became suspicious of him. Despite his protests of innocence, the authorities arrested him and sentenced him to be hanged.

Before his execution the man asked to be taken to the judge who had found him guilty. The judge was having dinner with some friends when they arrived at his house. The stranger once again said that he was innocent. Pointing to the roasted chicken on the table, he said, "As sure as I am innocent, that rooster will crow if I'm hanged."

Everybody laughed, but they did not eat the chicken to make sure. What seemed impossible actually happened. When the man was hanged the rooster stood up and crowed. The judge now believed the man and rushed to the gallows. Luckily, the rope around the man's neck was not properly tied, so he escaped from being strangled.

The man was released, but returned some time later to build a monument to the Virgin Mary and Saint Tiago, his patron saint. The rooster has since become a part of Portuguese folklore, a symbol of justice winning on behalf of those who fight for it.

# BEHOLD THE MIRACLE OF MOURE

*A church in the town of Moure attracts its own pilgrims with reported sightings of the shadowy top half of Christ, an annual incident since 1996.*

IF YOU WANT TO SEE A MIRACLE, head for the Igreja de Moure, four and a half miles southwest of Barcelos. This church in the little town of Moure has become a minor center of pilgrimage since May 18, 1996, when a ghostly shadow that is said to look like the top half of Christ first appeared. People have shot marvelous photographs of what is supposedly the Shroud of Jesus Christ. The head of Jesus wearing a crown of thorns has been seen on a communion wafer. Hundreds of the faithful gather to see the pale and sad face of Jesus on the wafer.

The miracle has since returned every year on May 18. During its 1998 appearance people circled the image; some clapped, while others begged for forgiveness for their sins.

There are also people who do not believe this to be true. Among them is the Archbishop of Braga who dismissed the miracle, saying that it is just an event that people imagine, and it can be explained through science. Further scientific tests concluded that the "miracle" was caused by a trick of light. However, science has not discouraged the faithful, who still flock here every May to witness what the people of Portugal call the "marvelous half-bodied manifestation of Moure."

# FESTA DE SÁO JOÁO

*The biggest festival in Porto coincides with the summer solstice in June. People dance through the streets, bonfires are lighted, and a huge fireworks display is staged.*

From all over the country crowds of Portuguese living in the countryside arrive in the towns to join the festivities that are held in honor of Saint John (Sáo Joáo in Portuguese).

The festivities are most colorful in Porto. In every corner of the city there are *cascatas* (arrangements of religious motifs). Music, lights, dancing, and songs keep spirits high until the early hours of the morning.

A bonfire is lit on the eve of the feast to drive away bad spirits and their bad influences on the land. At the same time, Portuguese drums are sounded to invite people to dance the *kola*, and in tents people eat traditional Portuguese specialties, such as *caldo verde*, strings of popcorn, and peanuts, which are popular with children, who take them home as souvenirs of the pilgrimage.

There is a Portuguese folk story about Saint John, who lived in 16th-century Portugal and Spain. One day while traveling, he came across a small child with no shoes. Since his own shoes were too big for the child, Saint John carried the boy on his shoulders. While stopping for a drink of water, the child showed himself to be the Infant Jesus and gave John a pomegranate, the fruit of the region, which has now become a symbol for charity.

*Some people have fun fortunetelling with eggs in water and playing cards; others carry leeks and small plastic hammers to "hit" others they find in the streets.*

# CALDO VERDE

## SERVES 6

*3 cups water*
*4 oz smoked garlic sausage (such as*
*linguica or similar)*
*1 ¹/₂ lbs russet potatoes, peeled, sliced*
*4 cups canned chicken broth*
*1 large bunch of kale (stems removed and*
*leaves thinly sliced)*
*2 tbsps olive oil*

**1** Bring 3 cups of water to boil in a large saucepan. Pierce sausage several times with a fork, and add to the water. Poach for 15 minutes.

**2**. Remove the sausage, but leave the hot water in the pan. Cut the sausage in half lengthwise, then cut again crosswise into ¹/₄"-wide slices. Set aside.

**3** Add potatoes and broth to the water. Simmer for about 25 minutes until potatoes are tender. Transfer half of the potatoes and the soup to a food processor, and purée. Return the purée to the saucepan.

**4** Add the kale and oil, and simmer for about five minutes until kale is tender. Mix in sausage, and heat again before serving.

# FESTAS GUALTERIANAS

**The annual Festas Gualterianas is one of Portugal's most famous festivals. It features a huge country fair, colorfully decorated streets, and processions.**

Portuguese food and wine are among the main attractions in Portugal. There is no better festival to show the country's best food than the Festas Gualterianas held in the ancient town of Guimarães. Since the first Gualterianas *romaria* was held in 1452, the large-scale celebration has been taking place on the first weekend of August every year.

The town has a special place in the story of Portuguese nationhood. It is the birthplace of King Afonso Henriques, who is known as the first king of Portugal. It was also the first capital of the new kingdom of Portucale (the

*Portuguese artisans display their striking handicrafts during this festival. On the right is an azulejo tile showing a traditional Portuguese windmill. Windmills have been used in Portugal since the 12th century.*

country's name in ancient times). It was from the town of Guimarães that King Afonso began taking over the country from the Moors and later created a united country, which is called Portugal today. Although Guimarães later lost its great status to Coimbra — which became the Portuguese capital in 1143 (Lisbon is now the capital of Portugal) — it is still very important.

There are still many medieval monuments along the streets of Guimarães, which many tourists come to see.

The crowd of visitors to Guimarães increases during the Gualterianas weekend, when thousands arrive for the most major event in the town. Festas Gualterianas is a *romaria* held in honor of São Gualter, or Saint Walter. It is especially lively at the exciting country fair, which takes place in the heart of the town. Stallholders from all over the country arrive to sell their goods. This is the time to see the country's best artists sell their masterpieces. Shoppers out for a bargain also make it a point to pick up beautiful paintings and Portuguese specialty candies and snacks at the fair. Children have an equally good time since entertainers dressed as colorful creatures from local folk tales walk along the streets to hand out balloons and sweets.

*People dressed in traditional costumes celebrate with music, dancing, feasting, and drinking.*

# MAKE YOUR OWN AZULEJO

## YOU WILL NEED

*1 unpolished white tile (6 inch square)*
*Oil paints*
*Thick paintbrush or sponge*
*Tracing paper*
*White paper for drawing*
*Pencil*
*Carbon paper*
*Glaze*

**1** Trace the outline of the square tile on a piece of white paper.

**2** Create a design you would like for your tile, using swirls, patterns, or anything you like. Once you have completed this, trace out an identical image of your design on a piece of tracing paper.

**3** Align the tracing paper onto the tile with the carbon paper in between. Go over the markings on the tracing paper again, pressing down hard on each stroke. The design that you created should be copied on the tile.

**4** Paint the tile in colors that you like with a thick paintbrush or sponge.

**5** Once completed, allow the paint to dry in a cool place for about five hours. Ask an adult for help to coat the top surface of the tile with glaze.

# FESTA DOS OCEANOS

**Nautical Portugal holds the Festival of Oceans to celebrate the success of the country and its people.**

The Festival of Oceans is held for two weeks every August to honor the country's rich seafaring history. Nautical parades, exhibitions, food fairs, and films are very much part of the celebrations. It is a fun and colorful event in Portugal.

Children love to see the performers dressed as fantastic sea creatures walking down the streets in the day. The most amazing procession held during the Oceans Festival is the Opening Parade. More than 50 people dressed as sea creatures march through the port town of Tagus.

The participants are accompanied by musicians who mark the arrival of Adamastor, the mythical king of all creatures. The fun continues at night, when a group gathers in the Park of the Nations for the grand welcoming feast.

Amid the bright lights, music, dance, and fireworks the Adamastor rises from the waters of the Tagus on a platform surrounded by fire. The buildings along the riverbanks are lit in blue at the same time. The show continues with other characters of the troop acting out various stories.

*Portuguese fishermen row out to sea in moon-shaped boats to catch sardines, ribbon fish, monkfish, or tuna.*

After the Opening Parade the festival kicks off, and the waterfront becomes the setting for a national exhibition of traditional cargo and fishing vessels. All vessels docked in the Park of the Nations Marina are open to visitors during the Oceans Festival.

Sailing competitions are also held on the final weekend of Festa dos Oceanos.

# PASTÉIS DE BACALHAU (CODFISH CAKES)

**SERVES 10**

*10 oz salted cod*
*14 oz potatoes (of the starchy variety)*
*1 small onion, very finely chopped*
*2 tbsps finely chopped parsley*
*3 large eggs*
*Vegetable or canola oil for frying*

**1** Rinse the cod well to wash away some of the salt. Put it in a big bowl, and soak it in cold water. Change the water four to five times for a period of 12 hours (for very thin cuts of fish) to 24 hours (for thicker cuts). Before cooking, taste a few strands to make sure it's not too salty.

**2** Boil the potatoes in their skins. Peel them, then mash them, and set aside.

**3** Simmer the cod for 20 minutes in enough boiling water to cover it until tender. Drain, discard the skin and bones, and flake it as much as you can with your fingers. Then cut it to threads with a fork.

**4** Mix the mashed cod with the potatoes, and add the eggs one at a time. Then add the onion and parsley. The mixture should be quite stiff, enough to make a spoon stand up in it. If you find it too dry, add one or two tablespoons of milk. Allow this to cool completely before deep frying.

**5** With two tablespoons, shape the fish cakes like large eggs, and place in the hot oil (370 degrees), turning them three or four times to get them nicely browned. When cooked, lift them with a big fork or slotted spoon, and put them on a paper towel to absorb excess oil.

# BON VOYAGE

**_Prince Henry of Portugal played a large role in developing the country's maritime strength, partly by proving that people can survive a sea journey._**

PRINCE HENRY "THE NAVIGATOR" was surely the most successful sea voyager in Portugal's history.

He probably never sailed out of the sight of land and never went farther from Portugal than the closest shores of North Africa, but he fought a popular belief that no one could survive a sea journey. Just as lands in the extreme north of the world were said to be unfit to live in because of extreme cold, so lands to the far south were thought to be unfit to live in because of heat. Anyone who traveled south would eventually be killed by the boiling sea, so the local story went. But to people's surprise, Prince Henry not only survived the sea journey, he returned home with cargoes of gold and spices from foreign lands.

Prince Henry was born in 1394, the third surviving son of King John of Portugal. During his time Portugal became a major sea power because contact by land with other countries was hard. The country lies along the Atlantic coast of the Iberian Peninsula. Any travel to neighboring countries had to go through the hostile kingdoms of Aragon and Castile, and over the Pyrenees Mountains, which are a barrier to reaching France.

Prince Henry's first voyage was to Madeira in 1418. He then turned his attention south to find a way around Africa to explore its unknown coast. A team of cartographers made drawings and maps as they explored farther and farther south.

Portugal's maritime strength grew after Henry's death in 1460. His captains explored the Atlantic islands and the coast of Africa to a point never reached. By sending ships and soldiers to these foreign lands, he made Portugal into a world power, setting up colonies in Africa, India, and South America. Today Brazilians speak Portuguese because of Henry's adventures.

# CHRISTMAS

*Christmas in Portugal is celebrated in nearly the same way as it is in other countries, but there are also several Christmas traditions that are uniquely Portuguese.*

I n Portugal there is much excitement at Christmas owing to the large population of Roman Catholics and Christians. It is a day to remember the birth of Jesus Christ, and it is widely celebrated.

The Portuguese set up scenes of the birth of Jesus (or *présepio,* as they are known in Portuguese) in their homes. This tradition can be traced back to 1560, when the Jesuits built the first Christmas scene in Coimbra.

Other festivities range from decorating houses with dried flowers and lovely candles to decking Christmas trees with ornaments, such as stars,

# CHRISTMAS IS YOUR BIRTHDAY LORD

Christ - mas is your birth-

- day Lord, Je - sus Son of God

You were born in Beth - le - hem as God's gift to man

Lord we ce - le - brate on earth, your

glo - rious vir - gin birth. You we honor

and a - dore, now and ev - er - more.

little balls, knots, and colorful electric lights. Singing traditional carols, such as "Silent Night" and "White Christmas," and gathering for big feasts with friends and family are also ways Portuguese celebrate this day.

The Portuguese enjoy an additional feast, called *consoada*, in the early hours of Christmas Day. Extra places are set at the table for the *alminhas a penar* ("the souls of the dead"). In some areas it is a custom for crumbs to be left on the fireplace for these souls in the hope that they will provide a good crop. In ancient times seeds were left out for the dead so they could return with fruits and grains at harvest time.

In recent years the Portuguese have adopted the Christmas tree, both real and artificial, as part of their celebrations. On Christmas Eve the family gathers around the tree as they wait to attend a special midnight Mass called *Missa do Galo* (Rooster's Mass). After leaving the church, they return home for a meal of boiled codfish with potatoes, Portuguese beans in pure olive oil, and port wine. They also don't forget Christmas goodies, such as bread fritters and sweet vermicelli, which are delicious.

An important ritual on Christmas Eve is the burning of the *foguiera da consoada* (Yule log) in the fireplace and in churchyards before dinner. The family keeps the ashes and remains of the log. People sprinkle these ashes in the fireplace during thunderstorms since it is believed that a lightning bolt will not strike near the Yule log's ashes.

Santa Claus does not appear at all in Portugal's Christmas celebrations. Instead, the Portuguese children eagerly await the arrival of the Three Wise Men, also known as the Three Wise Kings. On January 5 the children clean their shoes and put them along windowsills and doorways. They then fill these shoes with carrots and straw before going to sleep. This is to draw the Wise Men's horses to their houses during the night. Early the next morning the children wake to find their shoes stuffed with presents, candied fruits, sweet breads, and other treats.

The holiday season ends on January 6 with the eating of the *bola-rei,* or "King's Cake." It has a small surprise, usually a bean, baked into it. The person who finds the bean in his or her slice of cake must pay for another cake at the next celebration.

# THE THREE WISE MEN

According to legend, there were three kings who lived in the east named Gaspar, Melchior, and Baltazar. Also known as the Three Wise Men or Magi, these men saw a bright star on the night that Jesus was born.

Since they had spent many years studying the stars, they knew that this was a sign that the King of the Jews had been born. The wise men then rode on camels and followed the star westward for a number of days. The journey finally led them to Bethlehem on Epiphany, the Twelfth Night after the birth of Jesus. When they found the infant Jesus, they kneeled and offered gifts of gold to him. They also presented frankincense and myrrh, which have strong, sweet smells and are often burned as incense.

The King's Cake tradition also has its roots in this legend. On Epiphany a group of cardinals in 14th-century France would hide a bean inside a cake, cut it, and distribute the pieces. Whoever had the bean inside his slice of cake would lead the Catholic church for the coming year. Making this decision on Epiphany was significant since it was the day that the Three Kings announced their loyalty to Jesus. This tradition later spread to Spain and Portugal.

# SAINT MARTIN'S DAY

**Saint Martin's Day is one of the most colorful Portuguese traditions. The festival is celebrated all over the country, as well as by Portuguese around the world.**

Saint Martin's Day in November is remembered as a time for winetasting. There is an old saying that goes: "On Saint Martin's Day go to the wine cellar, and taste your wine."

However, there is only one story supporting this connection. It is said that a French emperor invited Saint Martin, along with his monks, to a banquet at the Royal Palace. Saint Martin accepted the invitation but insisted that a few innocent prisoners jailed in Toulouse be set free. The emperor agreed. It was normal at that time for the host to offer the guest the first cup of wine. The guest would drink from the cup, followed by the emperor. Although Saint Martin was aware of the custom, he wanted to teach the emperor a lesson about being humble. He raised the cup, sipped from it, and offered it to one of the other monks instead of the emperor. The emperor bowed to Saint Martin as a sign that he accepted his lesson.

What might seem to be more believable is that mid-November is about two months after the grape harvests and a good time to test the year's yield. Neighbors greet each other with wine glasses in hand for two reasons: winetasting and to honor Saint Martin.

The festivities start in the afternoon, when people eat grilled chestnuts and drink *jerupiga* and *agua-pe* (Portuguese liquors). Children paint their faces with the coal used to grill the chestnuts. In the evening people gather to eat Portuguese fried stickleback fish (*chicharros*) with boiled potatoes and yams, chestnuts, corn, sweet bread, rice pudding, and homemade wine.

# WORDS TO KNOW

**Abstinence:** Doing without something; for example, not having food or alcohol.

**Cartographer:** A person who makes charts or maps.

**Colonize:** To rule another country or an area in another country.

**Consecration:** The act of a person dedicating himself or herself solemnly to a noble goal or service.

**Medieval:** Relating to, involving, or typical of the Middle Ages in Europe in the 8th to 12th centuries.

**Melancholic:** A thoughtful or gentle sadness.

**Moor:** The Moors in Portugal were a mix of ethnic groups—mostly Muslim Berbers from Morocco, but there were also many Syrians and even Egyptians.

**Nautical:** Relating to sailors, ships, or seafaring.

**Parish:** Administrative part of a diocese that has its own church.

**Pilgrim:** A religious devotee who journeys to a shrine or sacred place.

**Procession:** A group of people or vehicles moving forward in a line as part of a celebration.

**Reparation:** The act or process of making amends.

**Resurrection:** The rising of Jesus Christ after he was crucified on the cross.

**Rosary:** A string of beads used to count prayers to the Virgin Mary.

**Surrealist:** An early 20th-century movement in art and literature that tries to express the workings of the subconscious mind by creating fantastic imagery. The works produced often look odd or startling.

## ACKNOWLEDGMENTS

WITH THANKS TO:
David Yip, Daphne Rodrigues, Sukarti Darudi, and Eric Koh for the loan of artifacts used in the production of this book.

PHOTOGRAPHS BY:
International Photobank (cover), Sam Yeo (pp. 6-7, p. 8 bottom left, pp. 10-11, pp. 12-13, pp.18-19, p. 22 top, p. 30), and Yu Hui Ying (all other images).

ILLUSTRATIONS BY:
Cake (p. 1, pp. 4-5, p. 7) and Lee Kowling (p. 15, p. 25).

# SET CONTENTS